EXTREME
BREAKUP
RECOVERY

Jeanette Castelli, M.S.

Urbantex Publishing

Miami, Florida

USA

http://Extreme.Urbantex.com/

Cover Design by Urbantex Publishing (http://www.Urbantex.com/)
Cover Photo by Oscar Gras (http://www.GrasPhoto.com)

Urbantex Publishing is an imprint of Urbantex, LLC.
Workshop In A Book ® Trademark by Urbantex, LLC.

Urbantex Publishing
First edition.
Manufactured in the United States of America

To all of you
who believe that there are
better ways of using your time,
than crying over your ex.

I have to thank my ex,

without him in my life,

I can finally find

the love of my life.

J.C.

Preface

You don't need to suffer one more day over your ex! No matter how long you have suffered, it is time to give up the pain and open up to a life free of pain.

You may feel that you can't stop clinging on to the past, but by clinging on to the past you are stopping life. Life is change; people come and go in your life, and that is okay. As you grow, new people will come and some may leave. It is all for your own good.

The tendency to cling to the old and avoid change is a common human trait. Unfortunately, it is also a self-defeating and self-destructive habit.

I have seen too much suffering and pain from breakups. Friends, family members and acquaintances have gone through long periods of pain before getting over their exes. It took them a long time before healing their hearts and opening for love again.

From the outside, it was obvious that their exes were not the right people for them in the first place, or that their relationship had become stagnant and even sour. Finally the breakup occurred, followed by a long period of pain, suffering and ultimately a slow healing.

Years later, after the breakup, I found them happier than ever, with a loved one. That new person seemed to be almost a perfect match. Looking back into their lives, they realized that unless they went through that breakup, finding their true love would not have happened.

So, why couldn't they accept that this breakup was for their own good in the first place? Why couldn't they get over it faster, rather than taking months or years to do so? Why did they have to go through years or months of suffering? Why did they waste so much precious time of their lives?

Your Choice

After a breakup, everybody has two choices.

One, leave the healing to time. Two, take charge of the recovery process.

The first method will take a long time, pain and suffering before healing. It is slow and torturous.

The second method, taking control, will allow anyone to accelerate the healing process, learn fast and move on, leaving space to find healthier and more fulfilling love than ever before.

This book is for those who choose the second option. Using the Extreme Breakup Recovery method presented here, you will heal faster than you thought possible. Two realities make this method a very exciting proposition: First, it works; second, anyone can follow it and get results. All the people that have decided to use the Extreme method, experience a relief from the pain almost immediately, and can continue with their lives shortly after a breakup.

You too have a choice, use your free will to choose what is best for YOU.

Contents

Introduction

Extreme Breakup Recovery is what you need, to save yourself months or years of suffering over a terminated relationship.

The method presented in this book is not for people who want to suffer. The Extreme F.A.S.T. Method is the ultimate healing tool: a quick, productive, effective and confronting method to heal as fast as you can. The speed and depth of your recovery depends on you. This is YOUR process. This book will guide you step by step.

Be prepared to enter a journey that will take you into strength and self-esteem. Following the Extreme F.A.S.T. method, doing the exercises, worksheets, and reading the affirmations, you will get over your ex sooner than you think. You no longer *will be immobilized* by the breakup, allowing you to take control of your life again.

The special section, Extreme Deep Healing, features a powerful and proven method to deal with those deep, long-term or overwhelming feelings for your ex that just don't seem to go away. But they will.

Your Courage

It requires a lot of courage and strength to want to heal fast. It would be easier to follow the mass belief that after a breakup we will go through a lot of pain and suffering for years, or at least months.

However, you have made a different choice. You believe in your own capacity to heal fast, in your own ability to get on with your life as soon as possible. You don't want to waste precious time suffering and dwelling on the past. You want to get the love you truly deserve.

Know that your true partner is already on the way. The more you suffer and prolong your healing, the more you will delay his or her arrival.

Use This Breakup For Your Benefit

Use this breakup as fuel for self-discovery and personal growth. Use this book to guide you through the steps to heal as fast as you can.

A new level of self-esteem, passion for life, love and relationships await you. This breakup is only an experience that prompts you to look at yourself in a different light.

This book is filled with exercises and worksheets to help you go through each step fully. By answering the questions and following the instructions you will get answers about your ex, your pain and yourself.

I recommend that you get a Journal to write your answers and insights. I will refer to it as your HEALING JOURNAL, throughout the book.

Behind each painful experience in life,
lies a new level of growth and joy.

Workshop In A Book ®

This book is designed to be like a do it yourself workshop. Each chapter is a step by step workshop session.

The exercises and worksheets in this *workshop in a book®* are designed to lead you into guided self-analysis. This includes understanding the past, confronting the present and questioning some of your ideas about the future; all regarding your last relationship and your relationships in general.

The exercises and worksheets are meant as a self-help instrument to accelerate your healing process.

Your answers can uncover painful areas for you and uncomfortable feelings may arise. Don't be afraid if that happens. It is normal to cry and feel pain as you explore and resolve your past. That means you are growing and healing emotionally. It is like the muscles hurting after you exercise. It means that your muscles are working and the exercise is producing results. The same goes with emotional healing.

If you feel too uncomfortable for your own safety, then by all means look for help, therapy, counseling or coaching.

Extreme Breakup Recovery is also designed to be like counseling or coaching sessions. This system intends to provide as much opportunity for self-help as possible. Each particular step will explore what you need to understand and evaluate, and will ask you to answer deep questions regarding aspects of each step. It entails a hard look at yourself, your behavior and your emotions. This book is not intended to replace any therapy or counseling.

As you heal from your broken heart and get over your ex, you want to clean all of it, leaving no residues of pain in you. That is the reason why some of the exercises and worksheets require a deep look into yourself and your life. A permanent cleaning requires work and emotional commitment. By bringing your fears, joys and pains into play you can fully heal and get over your ex, preparing yourself for the love you truly deserve.

1

THE EXTREME
F.A.S.T. METHOD

The Get Over Methods

Getting over your ex can be a very rewarding accelerated process of self-discovery and empowerment.

In a short time, you can come out from being immobilized to creating a new beginning, using the Extreme F.A.S.T. method.

There are other ways of getting over a breakup. The main ones are Time and Running away.

You have the power to choose how you want to get over your ex.

Time Will Heal, But Very Slowly

Some people believe that *time* will heal their pain. They are letting chance take control of their healing process. Besides, time takes too long.

CASE STORY

The following case illustrates how time alone is a long path to recovery. Not a choice, if you want a FAST healing.

Jessica, a sales manager, broke up with her boyfriend of 4 years. He called her to confess he had been seeing someone else for some time. She was full of pain. For a few days she didn't go to work and she felt completely guilty that it was her fault.

She decided that there was nothing she could do to recover from the pain. She believed that only time could heal her. Many friends and family tried to take her out of her isolation and pain, but she had decided to take *all the time* she needed to heal. It took her two years before she could go on a date again.

The Runaway Method–Fake Recovery

Another method used to try to recover after a breakup is to run away from the pain.

Some people may try to forget all about their pain by using drugs, alcohol, casual sex, etc., as an avenue to escape the pain.

These behaviors are just "crutches." They mask the pain and many times create a lot more pain. These crutches are self-destructive.

Using self-destructive behaviors will only prolong the healing process and may cause long-term damage, such as getting a disease or getting into an accident. This is a form of punishment and denial.

When you can recognize that the pain you are feeling is temporary, and also an opportunity to grow, you will not need these types of behaviors.

Running away from the pain is also running away from the lessons.

Recognize your pain
as an opportunity to grow.

The Extreme F.A.S.T. Method

This method of recovery means going through the steps that are necessary to heal fully.

The faster you complete the steps, the faster you will heal and the faster you will transform your life. You will dramatically accelerate your healing process.

F.A.S.T. stands for:
Face It
Accept It
See The Lessons
Take Yourself To A New Level

Basically, you need to FACE what is happening now, and what you are feeling. You need to face that you are experiencing a real pain, due to real circumstances.

You need to ACCEPT that you played a part in the situation, and that you can do a lot to get out of it, while feeling stronger.

You then need to SEE THE LESSONS that this experience is bringing to you. The more lessons you can find, the faster you will heal. Also, the less probability that you will be attracting similar situations in the future. The reason is that you would have learned the lessons you needed.

The final step is to TAKE YOURSELF TO A NEW LEVEL. This is where you take more action in the present to be happier and more fulfilled, without depending on a relationship. By doing this and taking the time to discover what you really want from a relationship, you will attract it faster into your life.

Each of the following chapters will focus on each step. First, it will show you how to identify the facts or issues you need to be aware of. Then it will show you what you can do about your discoveries to heal faster.

The chapters will provide you with worksheets for self-analysis and interactive exercises. There are also affirmations to help you reinforce some of the concepts.

EXERCISE 1

What do you want to do to get over your ex?
Circle your choice, from the list below.

1. Take the long way, and suffer for months or years, by leaving it to time.

2. Avoid the pain and try to forget it by using self-destructive behaviors.

3. Take the Extreme F.A.S.T. way and get over pain and suffering while taking control of your life again.

  If you chose number 3, you are already on your way to healing.

WORKSHEET 1

Answer the following questions. There is some space underneath each question, but use additional space if you need it. You can answer the questions in your Healing Journal. Be honest with yourself. Only you are going to see the answers.

How many times have you gone through a breakup?

How long did it take you to get over each of them?

What did you do to get over them?

What did you learn from each process?

How long do you want to take, to get over your ex this time?

2

START HEALING NOW

After The Storm, Comes The Calm

Anger, suffering, loneliness, isolation, appetite problems, sleep problems, lack of energy and low self-esteem. This is the "storm." A group of feelings, emotions and behaviors that are overwhelming.

Understandably, this is a very hard time for you right now. But remember after the storm, comes the calm.

You will soon feel okay. All the negative feelings and emotions will transform into acceptance and hope.

You can change your healing process from a long painful one, into a fast, fulfilling and exciting trip into self-love and discovery.

Embracing Each Experience

Every experience we have, either positive or negative has lessons for us.

If we are willing to look at each experience as a learning ground, we will understand that we are only students of life.

Here we are on this planet to learn how to make ourselves happier and more fulfilled. We are here to grow, evolve and learn. Doubtless, every experience we have will contribute to our learning and our growth

Everything that happens in your life,
no matter how painful or bad it seems, happens for
YOUR GROWTH.

The Power Of Pain

Pain always shows us the areas that we need to change and look into for a deeper understanding, acceptance and peace.

Sometimes, only when there is pain, then we are willing or forced to look into an area of our hearts and lives, that may be full of fear, regret or stress. Once we can understand and accept our "dark" areas we will be free from them.

Consider the possibility that your pain is a blessing in disguise.

Pain is a loud signal
for change and for the need of a
new level of love and joy in your life.

CASE STORY

The following case is a clear example of how something that seems so bad for us, can actually be good. A breakup can actually help us direct our lives in the right direction. We can end up learning more about ourselves and finding a new love.

Paul, a 31-year-old financial manager from Australia, was in love for 2 years with Karen. Regardless of all his attempts it was impossible to develop a relationship with Karen. She was not in love with him and ultimately rejected him. Paul's world was devastated. He felt that he could never find love again or happiness in his life.

The pain was so intense and unbearable that he made the decision to leave America and go back to Australia. Paul had to stay with his family. He'd never been close to his family, but this time, he managed to resolve a lot of unfinished business and created a new level of family-love relationships. He got a job in a large corporation and was able to buy a house within a year. After a few months he met a woman. She had very similar interests and goals. They started dating.

Paul realized that Karen's rejection, something that was so painful, had been actually good for him. It was the fuel that helped him create changes in his life: changes that were necessary for him, yet he would not have taken the action to make them happen. Everything had worked better than expected for Paul, and the breakup was just a catalyst for his growth.

Looking Into The Storm

There is a long way and a short way to heal your heart, and get over your ex. In the long way, a typical healing process goes like this:

- You feel depressed, empty, upset, and hopeless.
- You don't seem to be able to focus on anything.
- You day-dream on how you could have changed the situation or what you could do now, to bring your ex back.
- You may fantasize about how this person will suddenly realize what he or she has done, and will come back to you.
- You probably cannot sleep well, feel regret and guilt.
- Your appetite may be affected as well. You may be eating too little or too much.
- You also probably walk around with a sad face. People can see in your eyes that something is not quite right, and may constantly ask, "Are you okay?"
- Your pain may be expanding to all other areas of your life and you may be ignoring very important things for you, like your job, friends or family.

- You may be thinking of doing foolish things to get away from the pain like drinking, smoking or taking excessive painkillers.

The pain in your heart is not an easy load to handle, and you may wonder if it will ever pass. You may feel that your whole life has been one painful experience after another. It may take you months or years to change those negative feelings and start feeling good about yourself again. Many chances and opportunities may pass by you, but you feel immobilized to take action. This is the generally accepted path to healing after a breakup. It pretty much sucks!

Fortunately, using the Extreme F.A.S.T. method will put a stop to all that, and put you into the accelerated path to healing.

Right now, you may be experiencing some of those reaction and feelings from the above list. If you are, that is okay. As you look at your feelings and emotions, you can understand yourself and then let them go. Let's do that right now.

EXERCISE 2

Go through the following list. Check the ones that apply to you. Don't worry if you check a lot of them. Even though you may feel some of these at this time, you will be able to change them.

As you work through your healing process, you will experience a change in what you are feeling at the present time.

PHYSICALLY YOU FEEL:

_____Loss of appetite

_____Loss of sleep

_____Excessive hunger

_____Excessive sleep

_____Difficulty falling asleep

_____Lack of concentration

_____Tension

_____Tiredness

_____Restlessness

EMOTIONALLY YOU FEEL:

_____Stress

_____Irritability

_____Anxiety

_____Anger

_____Guilt

_____Depression

_____Self-doubt

_____Low self-esteem

_____Confused emotions, finding difficult to know exactly how you are feeling.

_____High emotionality, feeling very sensitive and reacting emotional to almost anything.

_____Illogical thoughts and ideas, like thinking that your ex will come back any minute.

_____Crying Spells (crying inconsolably suddenly)

_____Memories of bad times appearing in your mind

SOCIALLY YOU MAY BE EXPERIENCING:

_____Isolation

_____Aggression towards others

_____Lack of attention to others

_____Loss of interest in social activities

_____Need to ask for advice all the time

_____Lack of patience with others

_____Irritability with others

OTHERS:

_____Smoking

_____Drinking alcohol excessively or more than normal

_____Having casual sex encounters

_____Wanting to have casual sex encounters

This list includes the most common reactions to a breakup. As you start healing, they will disappear from your life and they will be replaced by positive feelings, emotions and behaviors.

Calm Begins Now

There may be a lot of uncomfortable feelings, sensations and emotions that you are experiencing right now: This is the storm. Remember that after the storm comes the calm.

Decide right now that you are too important and valuable, to let any of these feelings, emotions or behaviors control your life. It is okay to have all the feelings and emotions that you are experiencing, but you don't have to give up your life just to feel your pain.

*You need to take special care
of yourself during this time.
Be especially gentle, caring and attentive
to your own needs.*

WORKSHEET 2

Answer the following questions:

How would you feel, if you were completely over your ex? How would you feel if you did not have any pain from the breakup?

Write your answers in present tense. Use your Healing Journal if you need extra space. Use the guidelines below to help you with your answer.

PHYSICALLY I FEEL:

EMOTIONALLY I FEEL:

SOCIALLY I FEEL:

3

FACE IT

Just Face It

The first step in the Extreme F.A.S.T. method to get over your ex, is to face what had happened and what is happening now. By doing this you will feel better *immediately*.

The alternative to facing it, is *denying it*. Even though denial is a "natural" stage in any healing process, it is unnecessary and it only creates prolonged suffering. Denial can include behaviors such as thinking that the breakup is only temporary or not thinking about the situation by getting drunk.

You can accelerate your healing process by facing what you need. It will probably hurt, but it will feel so good afterwards.

Here is what you have to face:

- You have been hurt.
- You are emotional.
- You feel angry and guilty.
- You feel lonely and empty.
- You may feel powerless and hopeless.
- It is over.

Face It, You Have Been Hurt

There is a real reason for your pain. Someone has hurt you. Whether you have been rejected, or betrayed, or not loved back, you have been hurt by someone else's behavior.

It could have been unintentional, but nevertheless you have the right to feel hurt. It is only human to feel pain and many other emotions when we have been hurt. You are not a robot that can just discard a situation or be neutral to other people's behaviors towards you. Your ex hurt you. The breakup hurt you, even if you took the initiative.

Face It. You have been hurt. It is the truth.

Do not feel guilty about feeling hurt.
Be supportive and understanding with yourself.

Face It, You Are Emotional

After an event like a breakup, no one can be entirely rational. Your emotions are confused, mixed or out of control.

You may be feeling anger, pain, guilt, loneliness, sadness, and many other emotions. All of these emotions operating at the same time, create a very difficult terrain for rationality.

You may find yourself thinking very distorted thoughts. For example, one minute you may find yourself thinking of the many ways of getting back with your ex. The next minute on a plot for revenge.

Face it, you are more emotional than rational at this time, and it is okay.

Face It, You Feel Angry And Guilty

You have the right to feel anger. Anyone in your situation would. It is only a natural reaction to what happened to you. You may feel anger towards your ex, as well as towards yourself.

Your reasons for being angry with your ex may include: causing you pain and suffering, betraying you, lying to you, replacing you, treating you badly, and so on.

Also, there are many reasons why you may feel angry with yourself. Angry for having believed in this person, for having loved him or her, for having done what you did, or said what you said.

You may want to take some actions to heal your anger, such as calling and insulting your ex, or getting even. However, it is better not to take any actions out of anger, as they may not be the best for you and you will probably end up feeling worst.

Besides anger, you may be feeling guilty. There may be something you said or did in the past that you feel could have contributed to the breakup. The truth is, it takes two to make a relationship work or not work.

EXERCISE 3

In a scale from one (1) to ten (10), grade your anger.

One (1) is Not Angry At All, ten (10) is Extremely Angry.

I am this angry with my ex: _____

I am this angry with myself: _____

You may find that your anger is directed towards you, as well as your ex.

See the difference in scores. Who is your major anger directed to? Why?

You can start letting go of any anger towards yourself. You did the best you could or the best you knew how. You can't change the past, but you can create a new present and future.

Face It, You Feel Lonely And Empty

If you are no longer with your ex, you will feel lonely. After all, being with someone creates a habit, and you tend to get used to their company. Now you have more free time, and more time to be with yourself. The problem is that right now you may not want to be alone.

Being alone at this time makes you feel sad and depressed, because it makes more obvious the fact that you no longer can count with this person in your life.

Be compassionate and warm with yourself.
Count yourself as a friend.

EXERCISE 4

Take a few moments to feel the loneliness and emptiness you are now experiencing. How do you feel right now? Grade your loneliness in a scale from one (1) to ten (10). One (1) is Not Lonely At All, ten (10) is Absolutely Lonely.

I feel this lonely: _____

If you are too close to 10 (feeling absolutely lonely), make a list of the people you can count on right now, whether they are friends, family or co-workers.

These are the people I can count on:

If you have nobody you can count on, maybe it is time to look for support groups within your community. You can look for a list of groups in the local phone book and newspapers. You deserve to have supportive people in your life, start by giving yourself the opportunity to meet them.

Face It, You Feel Powerless

When someone hurts us, we cannot change what he or she did to us. As much as we would like to do something, we cannot do anything to change the feelings and behaviors of the *other person*. That lack of control will naturally make us feel powerless and vulnerable.

You probably feel that you have been hurt many times during your life and may even believe that you will get hurt again. The reason for that "selective memory" is that when we are hurt, we tend to focus on the negative experiences and enhance our own pain. We tend to remember and focus on those "bad" times almost exclusively.

Past, present and future may all *seem* dark and scary now, full of pain and hopelessly empty for you. This is just an illusion.

The truth is, you will feel better and the pain will pass. You are already taking the action towards your fast healing, and you should feel proud of yourself. You may be powerless over others, but you have power over your life and you are responsible for your well-being.

Face It, It Is Over

You may not be able to face it fully at this moment, but at least acknowledge that the relationship is over, as you know it. Whatever happens from now on, it is going to be different from the way it was in the past.

So face it, *it is over.*

As painful as it is right now, there is good news! Now you have opened the doors in your life for someone who can fully appreciate and love you. You have especially opened the doors for your self-discovery and growth. That is a major step.

> *Whatever is not for your own good*
> *will leave your life, and open space*
> *for something better to come.*

Conclusion

You have just completed the most important step in getting over your ex. Facing it, is a major accomplishment. This is the first step and it propels your healing. The first step is always the hardest and you are completing it. You are doing a great job!

Lets look at what you just faced:

- You have been hurt.
- You are emotional.
- You feel angry and guilty.
- You feel lonely and empty.
- You feel powerless.
- It is over.

Here are some suggestions to allow yourself to assimilate what you have faced.

Express your feelings and emotions privately.

Cry, scream and physically take it out (i.e. punching a bag or a pillow) in a *safe* environment, like your room or in your house. Express those feelings of anger, sadness and desperation.

Give yourself the uninterrupted time you need to take it out. You could write or talk to a friend about what you are feeling. The main thing is for you to express as much as possible without holding back. This experience will be very cathartic and healing.

Avoid self-destructive behaviors.

Decide that you are not going to cause any damage to yourself, because of someone else. Self-destructive behaviors are against yourself and can cause you physical and emotional damage, for instance, isolating yourself or exercising excessively.

Be your best friend.

Even if you have a best friend or friends, you still need to be your own best friend at this time.

Be compassionate, understanding and warm with yourself. Say nice and supportive words to yourself like "Everything will be okay," or "I am a lovable person."

If you feel like blaming yourself right now, stop!. Now, it's time to be caring and loving to yourself. Do nice things for yourself, like watch your favorite movie, or read a nice book. You would go out of your way if your best friend were in need, so do it for yourself.

WORKSHEET 3

Think of your relationship with your ex. How was this relationship for you?

In the columns below write the positive and the negative points. Write as many as you can. After you finish look at the two columns. Notice anything? What does it tell you about your relationship with your ex?

This list may continue to expand little by little, as you continue reading the book. As you make a new discovery of a positive or negative point write it down. By the end of the book you may have a long list to look at.

NEGATIVE   POSITIVE

WORKSHEET 4

What would you have liked to change in this last relationship? How could this relationship have been better? Write down your answers below, or use the Healing Journal.

Things I would have liked to change:

My relationship with my ex could have been better if:

WORKSHEET 5

Write a letter to your ex, just for you to see.

    This exercise is for you to be able to express all your thoughts and feelings in a safe environment. This will aid greatly in taking it all out. Don't judge what you write, and just let yourself go. Notice how your feelings or thoughts may change after the exercise.

4

ACCEPT IT

Just Accept It

After facing it, the second step in the Extreme F.A.S.T. healing process is acceptance. It means to surrender to what is real, versus to what we *wish* were real.

Acceptance, also means that we can look into ourselves for honest answers. We can see how we contributed to the situation and how we were partly responsible for it. Accepting responsibility for what happens in our lives, gives us a lot of freedom and more control, than when we look for someone to blame.

Here is what you need to accept:

- You have idealized your ex.
- You are giving more importance to your ex than to yourself.
- You were focusing a large part of your life on your ex.
- There were "warning signs".
- Suffering helps you avoid your life.

Accept It, You Have Idealized Your Ex

When we are in love, and especially if it is an *impossible* love, we tend to idealize the other person.

Many times we see them so ideal, that we even think they have special powers or a special magic. We may think that everyone else thinks the same way about him or her. Of course, being rejected in some way by such an ideal being, only will make us unworthy and miserable.

For some of us, there is a tendency to see the other person almost like a "saint" in terms of perfection and charm. I call this the **Saint Syndrome.**

THE SAINT SYNDROME

This syndrome refers to the fact that we idealize a person so much that only a "saint" could compete with them. Through our distorted eyes, they are perfect, gorgeous, funny, powerful, attractive to everyone, geniuses, and ideal in every sense. It seems almost overwhelming to have to deal with such perfection.

In order to heal fast, you need to bring the saint down to earth. You need to change that idealized image as soon as possible, because that will only prolong your pain.

How to bring the saint down to earth.
- Start by finding one thing that you didn't like about your ex. It could be a small thing, like the way he eats. It could be a major thing like the way she treated you in front of her friends.
- Now, take that issue and exaggerate it. See him turning into a cow and eating like one. See her turning into a giant mouth in front of her friends as she talks about you. Go along with it, exaggerate these images as much as possible and stay with these images for a while. Write it down if you want.

- Notice how your perception and feelings start to change. Doesn't your ex suddenly appear more human, or even a bit faulty?
- You did great! You have brought the *saint* down to earth.
- Use these process any time that you are feeling sorry for yourself.

Accept It, You Are Giving More Importance To Your Ex Than To Yourself

Probably, you are considering your ex's opinions as more important than yours. It is a need for approval. It works like this: if they approve and accept us, we feel good about ourselves. If on the other hand, they reject or criticize us, we feel lousy about ourselves.

Whether you feel good about yourself or not, it is going to affect how you feel about everything else in your life.

So, accept it. You may have been giving more importance to what your ex said about you or did to you. But now you know that your opinion is really the important one.

Can you find 3 great things about yourself right now? Say them out loud.

See how the way you feel about yourself is all up to you. Other people's opinions can affect us only if we give them more importance than to our own opinion. The best thing you can do is to constantly keep a high opinion of yourself.

You are the only one who can determine
to feel good or bad.

Accept It, You Were Focusing A Part Of Your Life On Your Ex

Before you had the breakup, your ex probably filled your time. You were going out, spending time together or just thinking a whole lot about him or her. So when you no longer have this person, your time feels empty.

In terms of the future, you may have even planned to spend the rest of your life with this person. You may have dreamed of the future perfect moments of an endless relationship. Walking on beautiful beaches, kissing in the mountains, marrying, having children, etc. Sounds like a movie?

You may have been expecting this person to fulfill all your needs for love, affection, approval and support. When the dreams are shattered, you feel hopeless about your future life and especially about finding love.

Right now, you have to accept that the perfect future you envisioned with this person, will probably never happen.

Accept It, There Were "Warning Signs"

In many cases, the situation that led to the breakup is not the real cause of it. Before that final breakup, there were warning signals that the relationship was not working well.

For example, you may have felt that your ex was lying to you, or that he or she was distant. Maybe it was just a "gut feeling" that something was not right. It is important for you to acknowledge that there were signals that you probably ignored. You may have had good reasons to ignore them, like protecting yourself from the pain or hoping they were not true. Don't beat yourself up for this.

Recognize that you have a very good instinct or warning system and you need to listen to it.

Below, list some of the warning signs that you experienced in your last relationship. Did you ignore them? Why?

Accept It, Suffering Helps You Avoid Your Life

Your life may be dull, boring or not the way you want it to be. So, you need a little drama. Delaying your healing by suffering after a breakup, could be a good way of bringing in the drama. By doing so, you keep your focus *only* on this painful area of your life: your broken heart.

When we focus on only one area of our lives at the expense of other areas, the consequences can be very negative. We can be letting opportunities pass by. We can start creating or having serious problems. We can end up being fired, loosing our friends, not finishing our projects, loosing money, clients, etc.

It is important that if you are adding drama to your life right now, you accept it. You may not "dramatize" consciously, but still you may do it. It is a normal response to protect yourself from pain and suffering. It doesn't mean that you need to stay in the drama, you can accelerate your healing by coming out of what I call the **Soap Opera Syndrome**.

THE SOAP OPERA SYNDROME

Why do we like to suffer so much? We seem to find a secret pleasure in seeing our lives like a TV drama. We enjoy suffering and drooling on our pain, because that creates a sense of meaning in our lives.

The dramatic suffering makes us victims and martyrs. That is the perfect excuse not to pay attention to the rest of the world and to the rest of our lives. After all, how could we go on with this painful heart?

Work becomes insignificant, friends are meaningless, or ideas and projects are nothing compared to the suffering of our hearts.

If you recognize this soap opera syndrome in your life now, let it go. Try seeing your love life as only one aspect of your life. That is all it is. Sure it is a very important area, but that is not all of your life.

Conclusion

You have just completed the second step in getting over your ex. Accepting it, marks great progress towards your healing.

Lets look at what you just accepted:

- You have idealized your ex.
- You are giving more importance to your ex than to yourself.
- You were focusing a large part of your life on your ex.
- There were "warning signs".
- Suffering helps you avoid your life.

You are doing a great job by taking responsibility for getting over your ex.

WORKSHEET 6

Understanding how you were a part of the problems of the relationship, helps you feel more in control. Write down five (5) things you can remember, that you were responsible for.

Example: "I was very critical of his friends." Or, "I did not listen to her problems."

1.

2.

3.

4.

5.

WORKSHEET 7

Imagine your life as a pie.

Draw a circle and label each slice after an aspect of your life. For example, Social, Work, Love, Finances, Family, School, etc.

See how your love life is only one aspect of it. Even if your love life is not fulfilling now, you still have other areas that are important in your life, and you need to give them your time and energy.

WORKSHEET 8

Rather than using your imagination to increase your pain, use it to reduce it. Instead of imagining years of loneliness and sadness to come, or dateless nights...
...Picture that:

- You don't feel any more pain
- You feel great about yourself
- You have inner peace
- You are very confident
- Your life is full of joy
- You have the love you want

5

SEE THE LESSONS

Learn Now

Life is always guiding us to what is best for us. Through the joyful and painful experiences that we live, we learn lessons that help us grow.

Sometimes the only way we pay attention to our deep needs, is when we experience pain and suffering.

Here is an example. You are here right now discovering more about yourself and what you want, because of this breakup.

These are the lessons you need to see:

- Your self-esteem.
- Your choice of a partner.
- The positive side (looking for the good in your ex).
- Your definition of love.

The best gift that you can give yourself is to see your lessons and grow from them.

Lessons About Your Self-Esteem

Most of us feel different when we are in a relationship, than when we are not in a relationship. We tend to feel better about ourselves if there is a meaningful relationship in our lives.

However, if your self-esteem depends on having or not having a relationship in your life, you may have to work on enhancing your self-esteem. When your value depends on having somebody in your life, you are basically giving your self-value to someone else.

Furthermore, even if you have a relationship, the quality of that relationship can determine how you feel about yourself. If the relationship is okay you feel good about yourself, but if there is trouble, you may feel bad about yourself.

If we depend on the relationship to determine our value, then our self-esteem is like a sailing boat in the middle of the ocean with broken sails and no engine, simply being taken by the currents.

CASE STORY

Karen was a professional artist. She was engaged with John, an architect. She broke up with him a few weeks before the wedding. John was constantly calling her names, and making her feel embarrassed. He would say things like, "You are putting on weight. You need to diet," or "You are a dummy, aren't you?" She would feel really bad about herself, sometimes for days.

At times, John would say positive things about her, such as: "Karen, you are sort of smart" or "You look okay" Then Karen would feel good about herself.

During the whole relationship, she was depending on John to feel good about herself and if his opinion was not positive, she would feel bad. She had to realize that she needed to build up her self-esteem.

It was painful for Karen to be honest with herself and accept her low self-esteem. She depended on someone else's opinion and she allowed her ex to put her down so many times. She learned her lessons and started to develop a stronger self-esteem, this time without depending on someone else's approval.

EXERCISE 5

Think about your last relationship and answer the following questions. Use your Healing Journal if you need more space.

How did you feel about yourself while being in the relationship? Why?

How do you feel about yourself now that you are not in the relationship? Why?

Compare both answers. See any similarities? Any differences? What does it mean to you?

EXERCISE 6

Write your answers to the following questions:

How do you feel when you are by yourself, that is, not in a relationship?

How do you feel when you are in a relationship?

How do you change when you are in a relationship? For instance "I become more confident," "I eat less," or "I become more insecure." Be aware of those behaviors that are not positive for you.

Look at your answers. See any patterns? What are the areas you tend to change more when you are in a relationship? What does it mean to you?

A Matter Of Respect

Another issue to evaluate is the respect that you received, asked for and had in this last relationship.

Respect is a quality of self-esteem. They go together. As you look at your relationship from the respect perspective you will learn about your own behavior, self-esteem and assertiveness.

In general, you can only get the respect from others in direct proportion to the respect that you have for yourself. That means that if you want others to respect you, you will need to respect yourself first, and then respect others.

When we are in a relationship, respect becomes a very important issue. We want to be respected and we want to respect our partner. But many times there are a lot of infringements to mutual respect.

Take a moment to think what respect means to you. What does it mean when you are in a relationship?

EXERCISE 7

Answer these questions:

Were there times when you felt that your ex did not respect you? What were those times?

What did you do about it? How did you handle the situation? Did you allow your ex to continue treating you that way? Or, did you confront the situation? Why?

Did you tolerate behaviors that you did not like, to avoid conflict? How did you feel about that?

EXERCISE 8

Answer these questions. Be as honest as you can with yourself. You need to take responsibility for your actions during the relationship.

Were there times when you did not respect your ex? What where those instances?

What were your reasons for not respecting him?

Look at your answers. What can you learn from your own behaviors?

Lessons About Your Choice Of A Partner

Have you ever wondered how we choose our partners?

There are too many theories. Some say we choose according to how we are. So we chose people that are similar to us. Other theories emphasize that we choose people that are opposite to us, or we choose people that compliment us. There are other theories that go from finding astrological explanations, to psychological profiles.

Regardless of the validity of those theories, the most important explanation of how you choose a partner is your own. Exploring the reasons of your choices, specifically of your ex, will provide you with a variety of lessons.

EXERCISE 9

Answer these questions:

Why did you like your ex in the first place? Remember when you first met him/her.

Was your relationship with your ex a "serious" relationship for you?

_____ Yes

_____ No

Why? When did it become "serious"?

How did you decide to get into a relationship with your ex? Why?

Look at your answers. What do you notice in how you choose a partner? In how you start a relationship?

EXERCISE 10

Answer the following questions:

In general, was your ex, similar to you or opposite to you? Why?

What common interests did you share with your ex?

What were your reasons for staying with your ex during all the relationship?

Look at your answers. Do you notice any pattern of how you keep a relationship? Can you see what is important to you in a partner and in a relationship?

Lessons About The Positive Side

Sometimes your initial judgment of a person has more to do with how you wish they were, rather than how they really are.

If your expectations about your ex were not met, you may have uncovered the truth about him or her. But it doesn't mean that there was nothing good. You need to look at the positive things this relationship left you.

Also, it is important to look into what you learned during the relationship, or what your ex taught you. When you recognize what the other person gave you, your negative feelings will diminish and you will heal faster.

As you appreciate what you have learned from your ex, you can let go easier.

EXERCISE 11

Answer the following questions:

What positive things did you experience during your relationship? Why where they positive to you?

What positive things did you learn from your ex? For example: "I learned to save money" or "I learned how to swim."

How did the knowledge that you got from your ex help you? For example: "I have better credit," or "I can enjoy the ocean more."

Lessons About Your Definition of Love

Each of us has a definition of love. Our definition of love includes beliefs, expectations and ideas about *love*. They all come into play when we are in a relationship.

Some of the beliefs come from your past experiences, like your family or past relationships.

Expectations come from your idealized image of love and relationships, that can come from your childhood dreams and fantasizes. It can also come from mass media concepts of love, like movies or books. Ideas about love can come from your own knowledge, education and philosophy of life.

It is important that you look at what you believe love is, what you expect from love and relationships. Whatever your definition of love is right now, determines in a great proportion what you get from a relationship. Take this opportunity to look deeply into your definition of love.

As you understand your definition of love,
you can change it, to get the love you want.

EXERCISE 12

Answer honestly for yourself:

Did you love your ex? Why?

Do you still love your ex? Why?

Look at your answers and see if you can see a pattern, or discover something about your capacity for love, your beliefs and expectations about love.

EXERCISE 13

Answer the following questions. Take your time to think about your answers. Use your Healing Journal to record your answers if you need more space.

What does *love* mean to you? What is your definition of *love*? Can you see where does that definition come from (Your parents, movies, friends, childhood, etc.)?

What do you expect from a relationship? How realistic or idealistic are your expectations? Where do these expectations come from (Yourself, your parents, friends, media ideas, etc.)?

What ideas do you have about love? What is your philosophy of love? Where does it come from? Do you like it? Would you like to change it? How?

Conclusion

You are well on your path of getting over your ex. Now, probably the intensity of the pain has diminished and you are gaining more control over your feelings and life. You are doing great!

Your answers to all the questions through the exercises as well as worksheets, have helped you discover major life lessons about your self-esteem, your choice of a partner and your definition of love

As you learn from these areas, you are growing and preparing to get the love you truly deserve.

After this breakup, there is something obvious: *You were with someone who was not meant for you as your life partner.* This is a great chance to ask: Is there anything that you fear about long-term relationships?

WORKSHEET 9

Remember what your ex used to say about you.

What good qualities did he/she point out?

What negative points did he/she mention?

Could there be any truth in his evaluation? Is there anything that perhaps you need to change?

WORKSHEET 10

Suppose for a moment, that you became famous five years from now; you were being interviewed in a famous night show. The host asks you about this relationship with your ex.

Host: A few years ago you were involved with _____ (your ex.'s name). Right? Tell me about that time of your life.

What would you answer?

WORKSHEET 11

The lessons in your choice of a partner, do not end with your ex. You must look at your previous exes as well (if any). Take a look at your other exes:

Is there a pattern in the partners you are choosing to be with?

What are the good qualities that all your exes seem to have?

What are the bad qualities that all your exes have in common?

Why do you feel you are choosing these people?

WORKSHEET 12

Visualize your ex(es) in front of you. Say to him or her:

"I forgive you."

"I let you go."

"Leave my life now."

"I wish you well."

Be aware of how you feel, during and after the exercise. Forgiving and releasing are major steps in healing.

6

TAKE YOURSELF
TO A
NEW LEVEL

Welcome To Your New Level Of Growth

The last step of the Extreme F.A.S.T. method, is to get to a new level in your life where you can start living in a more fulfilling way. Take this breakup as an opportunity to take yourself to a new level.

Many of the apparently negative experiences we have in our lives, guide us to explore new alternatives for ourselves. We may learn new ways of taking care of ourselves, new ways of feeling good about ourselves and new ways of relating to others.

By taking small risks that feel comfortable for us we grow and develop a new sense of self.

Your new level of growth will include new levels of:

- Self-esteem and confidence.
- Positive relationships.
- Passion and fun.
- Love in your life.

New Level Of Self -Esteem

After all the self-discovery that you have done throughout this book, you are now ready to enhance your self-esteem and develop more confidence. You now can learn to:

- Feel better about yourself.
- Know and accept yourself more.
- Be aware of your strengths and use them.

Self-esteem starts by knowing ourselves and appreciating who we are NOW.

Having a constant attitude of appreciation for yourself, is going to help you feel excited about your life. It is like having a best friend, all the time; supporting you and making you feel great. That is who you have to be for yourself.

*You need to appreciate yourself
for who you are now, in the present.*

EXERCISE 14

Write down 10 positive things about yourself.

Use "I am" or "I have" statements. For instance "I am intelligent," or "I have a great body."

After you finish, read them out loud. How does it feel?

1.

2.

3.

4.

5.

6.

7.

8.

9.

10.

Stop Fixing Yourself

We all want to change and improve in many ways, but we don't have to feel that there is something wrong with us, just because we are not as perfect as we wish.

A great way to create a sense of achievement and adventure in your life, is to determine which are those areas you are very good at, and practice them, instead of constantly "fixing" yourself.

When we need to be perfect to feel good about ourselves, we are simply not honest. We are never going to be perfect, but that is okay. We just need to be ourselves, with all the positive and all the not so positive. However, we need to appreciate our positive qualities *more* so they will grow and become stronger.

The more you focus on your positive traits
and what you do well, the higher your self-esteem
and confidence will be.

EXERCISE 15

Write down all the areas or things that you are good at. Use "I am good" statements. For instance, "I am good at organizing." Or "I am a good tennis player."

Write at least ten (10), I am sure you can find them. When you finish, read them out loud. How does it feel?

1.

2.

3.

4.

5.

6.

7.

8.

9.

10.

New Level Of Relationships

In order to get positive relationships in your life you first have to be clear about what you want. Many times we go around wanting something, but we are not clear about what is exactly what we want. Once we get clear, it is like a wish come true.

Relationships are not an exception. You need to get clear about what you want from a relationship, what you expect and what it means to you, before you can get it.

It is also important to understand the reasons why you want certain things in your relationship. As you look at your reasons you may discover that you have old ideas that need to be renewed. For instance, if you find yourself wanting a relationship that has no conflicts, then you need to reevaluate this. As you know, all relationships will have some conflicts.

As you gain clarity on what a positive relationship means to you; you will attract it easily.

EXERCISE 16

Make a list of 10 things that you *want* in your perfect relationship. For example: "I want it to be long-lasting" or "I want it to be romantic."

1.

2.

3.

4.

5.

6.

7.

8.

9.

10.

Now, try to see what is the reason behind each one of your wishes. Why do you want that trait or feature in your relationship?

Other Relationships

Romantic relationships are not the only ones that are important. Many of us tend to care so much about getting a partner, that we forget about other relationships that are meaningful.

Think for a moment, what are the meaningful relationships that you have. Do you have family? Friends? Co-workers?

Are you putting all these relationships in the back seat to a romantic relationship? Why?

Of course, finding your partner and developing a special relationship is important. But if you forget about the rest of the world, what happens if that relationship fails? Or what happens when you need a break from it? Or if you need to just share with others?

Also, it is a fact that having at least a few meaningful people in our lives tend to make us happier. So why not try expanding your circle instead of contracting it?

EXERCISE 17

List all the people that you have a relationship with. It could be friendship, family or work related.

After you finish, think of how important is each one for you. If they are very important, are you giving them your time? Or could you be giving your time to relationships that are unimportant?

Great Relationships Start Inside

In order to get the relationships that we want in our lives, we first have to start by giving ourselves what we expect from others.

You need to be like your best friend, your own partner, or soul mate. Not only will this help you to increase your self-esteem, but also this will accelerate the arrival of that special person into your life.

Love is the most powerful energy in the universe, and it starts by loving yourself. Take the time to appreciate yourself and give yourself love constantly. Trust that as you appreciate yourself, you will allow more good things to come into your life. Right now say "I love myself."

Your relationship with yourself is the most important. Now, is a good time to develop a more loving connection with yourself.

EXERCISE 18

Visualize yourself sitting across from you.

1) Say to yourself, "I love you."And keep saying it until it feels comfortable.

2) Thank yourself for your courage, persistence, and self-discovery.

3) Tell yourself that you deserve love and joy.

New Level Of Passion And Fun

Passion and fun are powerful energies that will bring positive growth and joy into your life.

When we are recovering from a breakup, we tend to forget about our passions and we stop having fun.

This is a critical time to revive your passions. As you do, you will pull yourself out of the pain and come out into the joy.

Passions can be what you love to do for fun, for entertainment or for work. For example, you can have a passion for business, a passion for roses, a passion for comedies. A passion is what you love to do, to have, to dedicate time to, because it brings you joy, not because you have to do it.

As you uncover your passions once again, you will realize that your time is very precious. You will use it more productively in following those passions, rather than suffering or waiting.

EXERCISE 19

List a minimum of ten (10) passions that you have. If you can't think of 10, then think about the ones you would like to have.

1.

2.

3.

4.

5.

6.

7.

8.

9.

10.

More.

A Promise To Yourself

Promise yourself to do at least one of your passions everyday from now on.

If there are some you cannot do easily, just take a step towards it. For instance, say your passion is to travel, but you can't do it soon. Go to a bookstore and look at books of places you would like to go, check the Internet, or go to a travel agency.

Take action on your passions. This will immediately make you feel alive and excited about life and about yourself.

As an additional benefit, when you are more aware of your passions, you will easily connect with someone who has the same passions.

Cultivate your passions.
As you do, you will create a powerful joyful energy
inside and outside of you.

New Level Of Love In Your Life

Love is energy. It is everywhere around you, not just in your relationship with a partner. Love manifests in many ways in your life. Think of the following expressions of love and how they apply to your life: (they are not organized in any particular order)

Loving your self

Loving your mother

Loving your brother/sister

Loving your best friend

Loving your friends

Loving a pet

Loving your home

Loving your memories

Loving your dreams

Loving your ideas

Loving your mind

Loving your spirit

Loving God

Loving a partner

Give To Receive

Make a commitment to yourself to be more aware of love and your unlimited capacity to experience it. When you focus even a little bit of your energy on giving love, you will receive more of it.

In general, our external life is a reflection of our internal life. So, if you give yourself more love, you will also get more love.

Once in a while, close your eyes and
send love to yourself,
everybody and everything around you.
You will receive more of it.

You Deserve The Best Partner

We all deserve the best partner. The problem sometimes, is that we don't know who is the best partner for us. We may focus on some features and qualities that are not necessarily the best for us.

If you have low self-esteem, chances are, you will get a partner that is not so good for you. That is why is important that as you enhance your self-esteem, you take time to clarify what your next partner would be like.

Right now, you have the chance to get a partner that is right for you. Dare to ask for the best, for your soul mate. Don't be limited by reality. Just for the fun of it, let yourself dream big. Dreams can come true.

Explore your expectations and wishes, around your ideal partner. Your soul mate is somewhere out there. Clarity will bring him/her closer to you.

*Having a clear picture of whom you want
in your life will bring that person faster.*

Conclusion

You have finished the last step in getting over your ex. By now, after following the steps in the F.A.S.T. method, you may feel that you are pretty much over your ex.

You are in the process of taking yourself to new levels of:

- Self-esteem and confidence.
- Positive relationships.
- Passion and fun.
- Love in your life.

From now on, your life can become a fulfilling experience of self-discovery. Life is like a big experiment, and you learn all the time as you experience your self and your life.

When you are ready to start dating or to taking your dating experience to a new level, you can read the book *The Joy Of Dating Again.* This book will guide you to create a joyful and self-empowering experience out of dating. (See more information at the end of this book.)

WORKSHEET 13

Think of all the people that are part of your life right now and send love to each one. Say mentally "I love you," while you visualize each of them.

WORKSHEET 14

Think of your ideal partner.

What qualities is he/she to have? What attitudes? What values? What knowledge? What activities would he or she have? What type of family? Write down your answers as follows:

- My ideal partner's values are:

- My ideal partner's qualities are:

- My ideal partner's activities are:

- My ideal partner's family is:

- My ideal partner's knowledge or education is:

- My ideal partner's passions are:

- My ideal partner's looks are:

Now think of the places where you could meet such person.

- I could meet my ideal partner in:

WORKSHEET 15

Think about what you have to offer in a relationship.

- I have the following passions to offer:

- I have the following knowledge or education to offer:

- I have the following values to offer:

- I have the following dreams to offer:

- I have the following qualities to offer:

7

EXTREME
DEEP
HEALING

You Deserve To Let Go

If you still feel deep emotional pain after completing the steps of the Extreme F.A.S.T. method, you need to do a deeper cleansing and releasing process. There may be a strong attachment to your ex, causing deep emotional pain in your life.

Emotional pain is generally accompanied by deep emotions such as melancholy, depression, regret and anger. There is a constant internal conflict caused by your need and desire to feel good and the pain caused by the uncontrollable memories associated with your ex. This conflict can leave you exhausted physically, emotionally and mentally.

At times, you may feel that it is hopeless to do anything, because you feel that there is no way you can eliminate those memories or even change them.

Sometimes you may find that the pain goes away and that you are able to move on; however, it only seems to be temporarily, because the pain seems to come back again and again. You wonder if you will ever be able to forget or remember without pain.

Don't despair. There is hope. First, you need to know and acknowledge that you deserve to let go. You don't need to be permanently attached to painful memories and experiences. It may be easier than you think to change these negative feelings, and to stop the conflict inside of you.

Decide right now that you deserve to let go and move on. You don't need those memories anymore. You certainly don't need the internal conflict nor the strong negative feelings anymore. You have better things to do with your life. You deserve to let go starting NOW. It doesn't matter how long you've been attached to the haunting memories of your ex(es); NOW is a good time to let go of the pain, layer by layer.

The Layers Of Deep Healing

When memories are so painful, we may wish we had selective amnesia, and forget certain times and people in our lives. Unfortunately, it is very unlikely to get such amnesia; but we can transform all the painful memories into neutral memories, that don't drain us emotionally.

How can you transform deep pain into neutral memories? By using the layer system to heal deep emotional pain. This system is nothing more than a process of healing layer by layer, until all the pain is gone. Each layer is different from the other, and include different elements that contribute to the pain.

When you work each layer and then let it go, you heal that layer; then you can move on to the next one, until all are healed.

Imagine that you need to get rid of a white onion. If you peel a few layers of the onion, you still have some more left. Only by peeling ALL the layers, you can get rid of the onion fully.

The reason why some methods of emotional healing seem to work, is because they heal one or two of the layers; however, if the other layers are not healed, then the pain will return.

I have uncovered four layers of deep healing; they are:

- Layer one: Positive Real Memories
- Layer two: Negative Real Memories.
- Layer three: Positive Imagined Memories.
- Layer Four: Negative Imagined Memories.

There is pain coming from each layer. The memories, imaginary situations and thoughts become sources of pain that can be identified and transformed.

As you work through each layer, you will heal all deep emotional disturbances. When you are done, the memories of your ex will just be memories such as your history professor in 8th grade, or a casual coworker from your last job. Believe it!

EXERCISE 20

Think of your ex. What are the first things that come to your mind? Write them down, whatever they are, don't judge any of them, write them down as close as possible as you are thinking or imagining them. If you need more space, use your Healing Journal.

Now look at what you wrote. Is it a real situation, interaction or moment that actually occurred in the past? Or, is it an imaginary situation of what could have happened, but in actuality never did? Is it positive? Is it negative?

See if you can classify those memories in one or more of the following categories:

- Real Positive Memories
- Real Negative Memories
- Imagined Positive Memories
- Imagined Negative Memories

Layer One: Positive Real Memories

When you remember the good times or the positive interactions with your ex, you may only be reinforcing the feelings of loss. What starts as a beautiful memory of positive past times, soon becomes a source of pain. After all you've "lost" these moments or "they are gone forever." You may even feel that you have lost the chance for happiness.

This is only an illusion.

One thing is certain: if you could have those moments in your life, you can have them again. Sure, they won't be the same, because you have changed, and your life circumstances have changed too. If you could have those positive feelings before, you can have them again with *someone else*.

Your life is not over, neither your desire for love and happiness. In order to move on, you need to let go of this layer by tackling each of its components:

1. The Perfect Moments.
2. Feeling Complete.
3. The "You are THE ONLY ONE for me" Syndrome.

Let's see them one at the time.

1. The Perfect Moments.

You remember those moments when you and your ex were laughing, kissing, playing, looking into each others eyes..., you know, the perfect moments.

You remember the perfect moments with joy and pleasure, but soon, reality kicks in and you realize that you no longer have them in your life (because you no longer have your ex). Then, those perfect moments turn into sour moments that remind you of loss, loneliness and pain.

2. Feeling Complete.

You may feel that you were complete with your ex and that now you are incomplete, because he or she is no longer in your life.

The truth is: you are complete all by yourself.

Some people can enhance your feelings of joy, happiness and self-confidence, but it doesn't mean you need someone else to be *complete*.

Of course, if you feel that your ex completed you, well, now you are "incomplete." Feelings of sadness, emptiness and regret may fill you each time you remember the "completeness" that you felt with your ex.

3. The "You are the only one for me" Syndrome.

When you feel that your ex, and *only your ex* was the only partner for you, you are making your life very hard. This person is no longer in your life and may never be again. You may think that from now on, anyone who comes into your life, can't and won't measure up to the standards of "THE ONLY ONE."

You may think you will find another person, but in your mind you may have already set up a standard impossible to reach by anyone else. Then, you will be disappointed with anyone who tries to come close to you, because he or she is not "THE ONLY ONE" for you.

This is another illusion. I will prove it to you. If you were born in another country, and were living there, would you find someone to love? Yes, you would. That means there are more than one "THE ONLY ONE" for you.

The perfect moments, feeling complete and the "you are the only one for me" syndrome, are all based on positive real memories. They represent moments and experiences that were good for you, but they hurt because they are no longer available to you, or at least that is what you think. The positive experiences are yours to keep, the feelings of loss and emptiness need to be released.

EXERCISE 21

1) Think of a great time with your ex. Remember the perfection of the moment. Resist any desire to feel the loss of those moments, just focus on the beauty of the moment. Say to yourself:

> "I deserved this moment of joy"
> "I deserve more of these moments of joy"
> "I created this moment of joy"
> "I can create new moments of joy"

2) Close your eyes and touch your heart.
Say: "I deserve to let go, I deserve to move on."
Visualize your ex in front of you. Say to him/her:

> "I am complete without you"
> "I don't need you to complete me"
> "You are not the only one for me"
> "I set myself free from you"
> "I now let go of my attachment to the illusions of you"

EXERCISE 22

Imagine the same great moment or situation from the previous exercise, with another person. It can be someone you now know, or just an imaginary person.

How do you feel when you replace your ex with someone else?

Release all the feelings of resistance and let yourself enjoy the moment in your mind, with someone else. See how you are the catalyst for your own joy. See how you can create the feeling of joy with a different person.

You are the catalyst for your own joy.

Layer Two: Negative Real Memories

The negative real memories are the negative situations and interactions that actually happened between you and your ex. These can be found at three different times: before the breakup, the actual breakup and after the breakup. Let's look at them one at the time.

1. Before the breakup

The negative experiences, moments and interactions that you had with your ex before the breakup may include fights, arguments, lies, deception, betrayal, infidelity, etc.

When you remember these negative issues, you can't help but feel negative emotions such as anger, regret, or sadness. You may even feel abused and used. Those negative feelings about yourself can only contribute to a low self-esteem (that feeling that you don't really deserve the best). Those negative feelings will make you feel as if you are stuck with negativity all your life.

Maybe you feel regret that you let those situations happen, and feel guilty that you were not strong or assertive enough to stop any type of abusive behavior. The truth is: you did the best you could at that time, and now you are free from those past negative situations with your ex. Your ex is no longer in your life and you have already learned precious lessons from your experiences before the breakup.

2. The Breakup

The memories of a painful breakup may be playing and re-playing in your mind: the things your ex said to you, what you said, the circumstances around the breakup, etc. All the pain associated with the breakup is like a traumatic experience for your heart and you need to heal it completely.

You may regret that the breakup occurred. You may feel that you could still be with your ex. The truth is: your relationship was not meant to last, and no matter what you would have done differently, it would have still broken apart. Maybe not at that moment, but it would.

3. After the breakup

You probably remember what you did after the breakup; like crying, calling on the phone a thousand times, getting drunk, being out of control, etc.

Replaying those memories in your mind will only increase your pain, and enhance your internal conflict. What you need to do, is accept that you did your best to handle the breakup. Accept that whatever happened is okay now, and release the need to change it.

EXERCISE 23

What were the situations with your ex that hurt you the most? Write down the top three.

Be aware that you don't have those experiences in your life anymore, they are gone, no longer in your life. You are free from those moments, they are only memories, and you can choose not to be hurt by them anymore.

Feel the relief that they are gone forever, and see how they belong to the past. Now, you are safe from that pain. The worst has happened already. You can now move on. You don't ever have to live or re-live those experiences in your mind.

You are free from any painful experience
from your past relationships.
You are free to create joyful experiences
in the present and future.

Layer Three: Imagined Positive Memories

The memories of beautiful things that never happen can be as real to us as the memories of things that actually happen.

You may imagine how wonderful your life would be if your ex were still in your life; and how many of the bad things you went, or are going through, would not have happened if that person were still in your life.

Realize that you are giving too much "imaginary power" to your ex. It is YOU, not the people you are with, that create your reality. The people around you can contribute or hinder your overall happiness, but they don't create it.

There are two categories in this layer: Useless Joy and Problem-Free Life. Let's look at each one in detail.

1. Useless Joy

You may experience positive things in your life, (such as travelling, opening a business, or getting a new job), only to find yourself thinking that the experience is not worthy without your ex.; or that it would be so much better if he or she were there with you.

You may miss a lot of chances to enjoy life by yourself, or you may avoid meeting new people, because your mind is stuck in the imaginary ideal moments that will never happen with your ex. In the meantime, your present life slips away.

Sometimes, you may even lose all the motivation to achieve anything in life. You may already have given up the excitement and challenges of your own goals, transforming your life into a survival experience.

It is as if the joy that you can create from positive experiences, meeting new people and achieving your goals and dreams is "useless." Unless you share it with someone, and preferably your ex.

Let's suppose for a moment that your ex was with you at those moments of joy or success. What makes you think that you would not be having a fight? Or that he / she would not sabotage you? Or be extremely jealous of you? The reality could be quite different from what you imagined.

Your idealized imagination can twist things around and make you feel as if you are missing something perfect, while leaving you with feelings of regret, sadness and disappointment. The best thing you can do, with these imaginary memories of ideal moments, is to eliminate them altogether.

You need to create new memories with real people or by yourself. If you think that you can't enjoy life as much, because you have nobody to share it with. Think again: You are *somebody*, and somebody worth sharing your joy with.

Trust me, another person will come along, but in the meantime why not enjoy your life?

2. A Problem-Free Life

You may imagine that if only (and only) your ex was in your life you would not be having this or that problem. You imagine your ex as some kind of "savior," saving you from many of the problems you are now having.

This is an illusion, a white lie, that you are telling yourself. It could be an excuse for your lack of action towards solving your own problems. How could you resolve the problems you have when you have lost such person? Your problems may become *insignificant*, yet they keep growing.

You may have an unconscious desire to be saved. Some people even go to the extreme of letting all the problems out of control, as if waiting for that "savior" to come. But it never happens. They end up in bankruptcy, losing a job, or sick.

Even when you were with your ex, you had problems; even if you were still with your ex, you would still have problems. There is no such thing as a problem-free life. You are using your ex as an excuse not to handle your problems or make the changes that you need to make in your life.

Those imaginary memories of being saved by your ex, can become excuses not to take responsibility and control for your life.

You can't afford to wait for your ex (or anyone else) to come and save you. You must save yourself, with or without a partner, with or without your ex.

EXERCISE 24

The Holiday Scene.

For many people who had a breakup, the holidays are the toughest times. If this is your case, this exercise may help you.

Imagine your next holidays with your ex. No longer are you alone and everything seems great. Now, introduce a new element into your imaginary scene. There is, your ex with his/her three worst qualities (remember them?).

Suddenly the lovely Christmas or New Year scene becomes a fight, or an alcoholics movie, or maybe it will turn into a jealous strike.

Oh, sorry to have ruined the holiday scene for you, but you are better off without your ex. Trust me.

Now, if you allow yourself, you can create new real memories that may not be perfect but they are real and fresh.

EXERCISE 25

List the areas of your life where you feel you have lost your motivation or are out of control. For example, you were working towards a promotion, but no longer care, or you used to exercise and now you just don't do it, or you had your finances under control and now they are a chaos.

Could these situations be caused by the loss of your ex? Are you expecting to be saved by someone? Is it your ex? Are you expecting someone (or your ex) to come and give you the motivation and cheering that you need?

Answer this: Is there a probability that someone (maybe your ex) will come and save or rescue you?

If yes, sit down and wait.

If no, decide right now that you are a complete person, an adult and don't need to be saved by anyone but by yourself. Start saving yourself NOW.

Layer Four: Imagined Negative Memories

In this layer you will find scenes with your ex that are negative, yet they never happened. For instance, you imagine that you called your ex, he hung up on you, and then you felt terrible. Or you imagine that you met your ex by chance, she insulted you, and you were embarrassed and humiliated.

These situations never occurred, but you are creating emotions and feelings that are real for you. By playing negative scenes in your mind, you create negative emotions and feelings that are just as strong as if the situations were real.

You may be, unknowingly, the one who continues the painful experiences with your ex long after they are gone in real life. Your imagination is very strong and creative, and you must use it for good. It is like Superman. Imagine if he was doing bad stuff instead of good. He would create terrible damage, but instead he does good. Your imagination: it is a powerful superhero, but *you* decide which way it works, for or against you.

This layer also includes the imaginary dialogues or conversations with your ex. You may have them constantly or only once in a while. These conversations are like having your ex in your head.

You are carrying a conversation, you are talking, arguing, sharing, all inside of you. This type of "dialogue" can be very draining for you. It generally carries a lot of emotions that are not good for you.

There is only one thing you can do with the cycle of negative imagined memories and the inner dialogues with your ex: break it.

Here are some ideas:

- When you start imagining being rejected by your ex, replace the scene with meeting someone really good looking and exciting. Who also happens to like you.

- If you feel sorry for yourself because you think of negative memories with your ex, see yourself as a strong and powerful person, pushing your ex away and out of your way as you say, "Excuse me, but you have to move, I have a life to live that doesn't include you."

- Each time you have an imaginary conversation with your ex, stop it and instead do something pleasurable for yourself.

Regeneration

You probably have heard about the Phoenix. This mythological bird must burn to ashes before it comes back to life, stronger and more beautiful than before.

As you burn to ashes all the memories, emotions and feelings that you once had for your ex, you regenerate. Your mind will be at peace and your heart open for life and love again.

You are more powerful that you think. You can transform your life and attract a partner who will enhance it; however, you need to leave the old behind for the new to come.

All the good that you experienced with your ex, is yours to keep, after all you co-created those experiences. Without you, the joy and happiness in your last relationship would not have existed. You have the capacity to do the same once again. You own the ability to create those experiences again.

Your ability to create and attract joy, love and friendship didn't disappear with your ex leaving your life, (or you leaving your ex). You still have that ability intact, and you can use it again. Allow yourself to do it. Allow yourself to break free and regenerate.

Totally Moving On

You are a very special person full of qualities and energies that are ready to come out. You deserve to go out into the world and share your uniqueness.

You can discover love anywhere, wherever you are. As you love yourself more and affirm your value, you will connect with people who will respect and value you.

When you are focusing in living your life joyfully, you will attract a partner sooner than you expect. Remember that you don't *need* anybody to be happy. You may prefer to have somebody, but you still deserve to make yourself as happy as you can be.

Congratulate yourself, and start enjoying your increased level of self-esteem, your passions and the new sense of love in your life. You will be amazed with the results and the new doors that will open for you. Celebrate life, celebrate yourself!

WORKSHEET 16

Fill in the blanks below with 15 things you like to do, or would like to do for yourself. Focus on your passions, your hobbies, and your dreams.

I will give you three examples, and the rest is up to you.

1. Take a bubble bath while listening to calming music; you can light up some candles and make sure that there are no interruptions.

2. Go to a funny movie with a friend and snack the whole time.

3. Take a class in something you have wanted to do, like cooking, meditation or horseback ridding.

4.

5.

6.

7.

8.

9.

10.

11.

12.

13.

14.

15.

GREAT JOB!

Now start doing them and have fun, whether you do them alone or with somebody.

After all, <u>YOU</u> are great company.

Inquiries regarding Jeanette Castelli's availability for personal coaching, group workshops, or to speak to your group, meeting, conference, or convention should be addressed to:

E-mail
INFO@Urbantex.com

About The Author

Jeanette Castelli is an expert in personal leadership, relationships and recovery. Her education includes a Masters of Science of Psychology in Mental Health, a Bachelors of Science of Psychology and a Masters of Business Administration.

In her trademark user-friendly style, described as a "Workshop In A Book ®," she introduces *Extreme Breakup Recovery.*

Based on her experience as a therapist and coach, and her own research, Castelli developed the Extreme F.A.S.T. method for breakup recovery. Her writing focuses on self-empowerment and learning through insight and action. She believes in "doing and not just reading," to create true changes in life.

Her deep emotional healing method, presented in the book *Extreme Breakup Recovery,* has proven to be effective, successful and permanent, in dealing with long-term or deep emotional pain.

In her book, *The Joy Of Dating Again*, you will discover the 21 Self-Empowering keys to create a powerful, transforming and joyful dating experience.

To contact the author, send feedback or comments:

E-mail at Info@Urbantex.com

The Joy Of Dating Again:
21 Self-Empowering Keys

by Jeanette Castelli, M.S.

The Joy Of Dating Again, is a book written especially for those going back to the dating world. There are 21 self-empowering keys that will help you uncover the secrets to enjoy and succeed at dating again. Here you will find the Personal Keys, Communication Keys, Social Keys, Joy Keys and Spiritual Keys, that you need to create the joy of dating again.

- Evaluates the myths of dating again.
- Addresses the unique issues and experiences of dating again, from personal to spiritual.
- Reduces the trial and error process of dating and helps you be in control of your own process.
- Presents the clear solutions for successful dating that are within your reach.
- Filled with specific personal strategies to get positive results and improve the quality of your life.

Special Features
- This is a do-it-yourself Workshop In A Book ®.
- Each of the 21 keys is based on self-empowerment. Designed to uncover your own power to create life changing results personally and in relationships.
- Interactive exercises and worksheets to help you enjoy dating again.
- Visualizations and affirmations to create faster results.
- Contains guided Social Experiments to take action immediately.

ISBN: 0-9742061-1-3

For information write to info@urbantex.com or visit website http://JOY.urbantex.com/

Printed in the United States
118567LV00003B/127/A